ELEMENTARY

Glover's Festival Of Favorites

AF881627

CONTENTS

Banjo on My Knee 18
Big Chief Thundercloud 8
Cathedral Chimes 25
Doo-Dad Boogie 12
Hep Kittens 20
It's a Game 6
Lonely 14
The Merry-Go-Round 26
Rodeo 28
Snap-To-It March 10
Sneaky Creeepy Things 4
Sugar Cookies 2
Sunrise 22
Sunset 24
That Place 30
Trumpets 16

Cover Design and Illustration: Joseph Klucar
Editor: Carole Flatau

Sugar Cookies

Happily

David Carr Glover

p
f

Sneaky Creepy Things

David Carr Glover

mp
r.h.
l.h.
rit.
mf
l.h.
f
r.h.
p

It's A Game

David Carr Glover

f
rit.
a tempo
L.H.
ff
L.H.
rit.
R.H.
mf
mp
a tempo
mf
f
mf
f
p
Quickly
ff
8va
8va

Big Chief Thundercloud

David Carr Glover

Moderately, never fast

f
mf
p
f
p
r.h.
l.h.
ff

Snap - To - It March

David Carr Glover

Lively

f
mf
l.h.
l.h.
p
rit.
r.h.
8va

Doo-Dad Boogie

David Carr Glover

Moderately

r.h.
mf
f
p
mf
mp
f
8va

Lonely

David Carr Glover

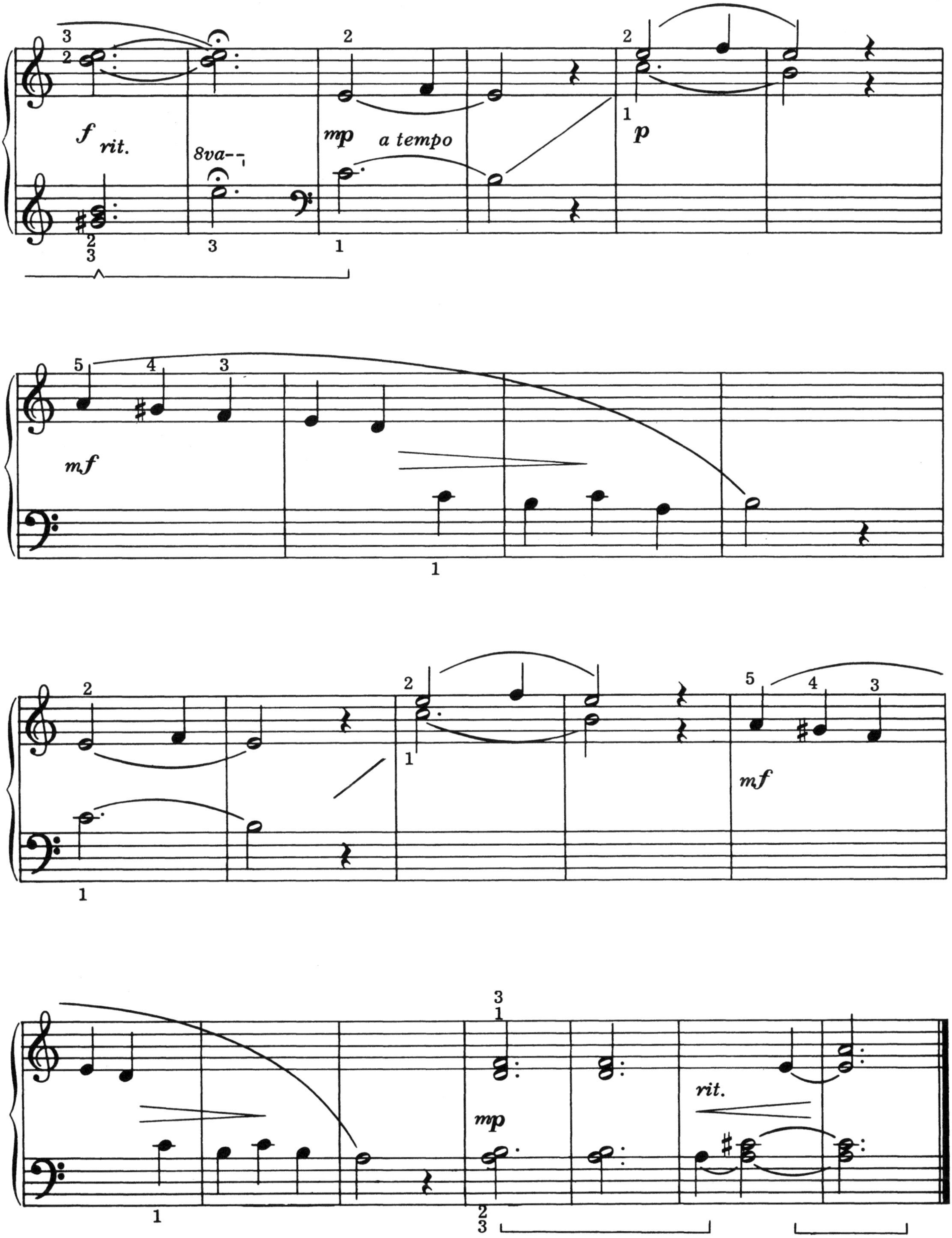
f
rit.
8va
mp
a tempo
p
mf
mf
mp
rit.

Trumpets

David Carr Glover

Briskly

mf
f
mf
f
p

Banjo On My Knee

David Carr Glover

Lively

mp
mf
mp
mf
mp
mf
f
mf
D. C. al Fine

Hep Kittens

David Carr Glover

f
mp
mf
mp
f
mf
p
r.h.
ff
8va

Sunrise

David Carr Glover

mf
l.h.
mp
f
poco a poco cresc.
rit.
p

Sunset

David Carr Glover

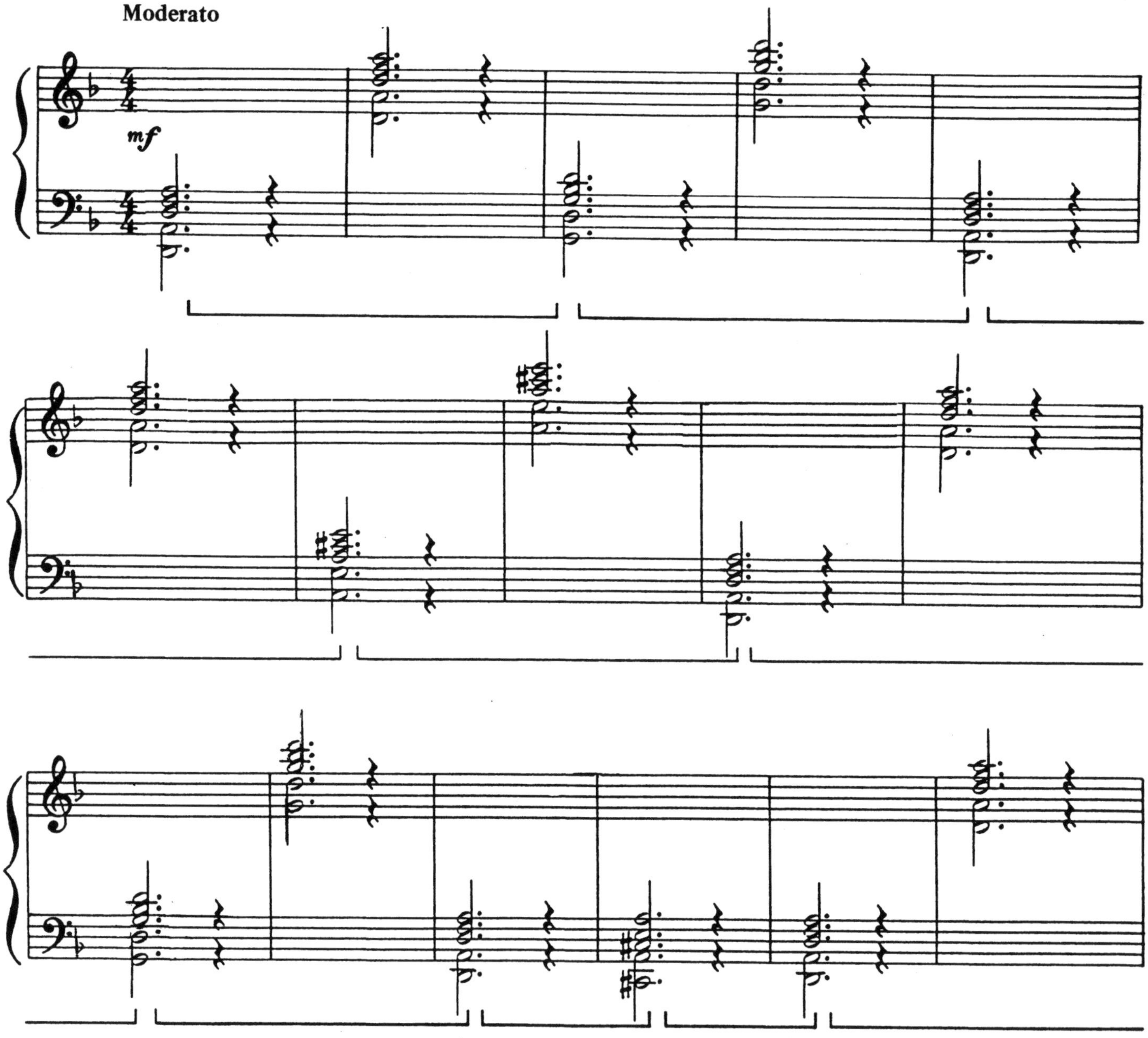

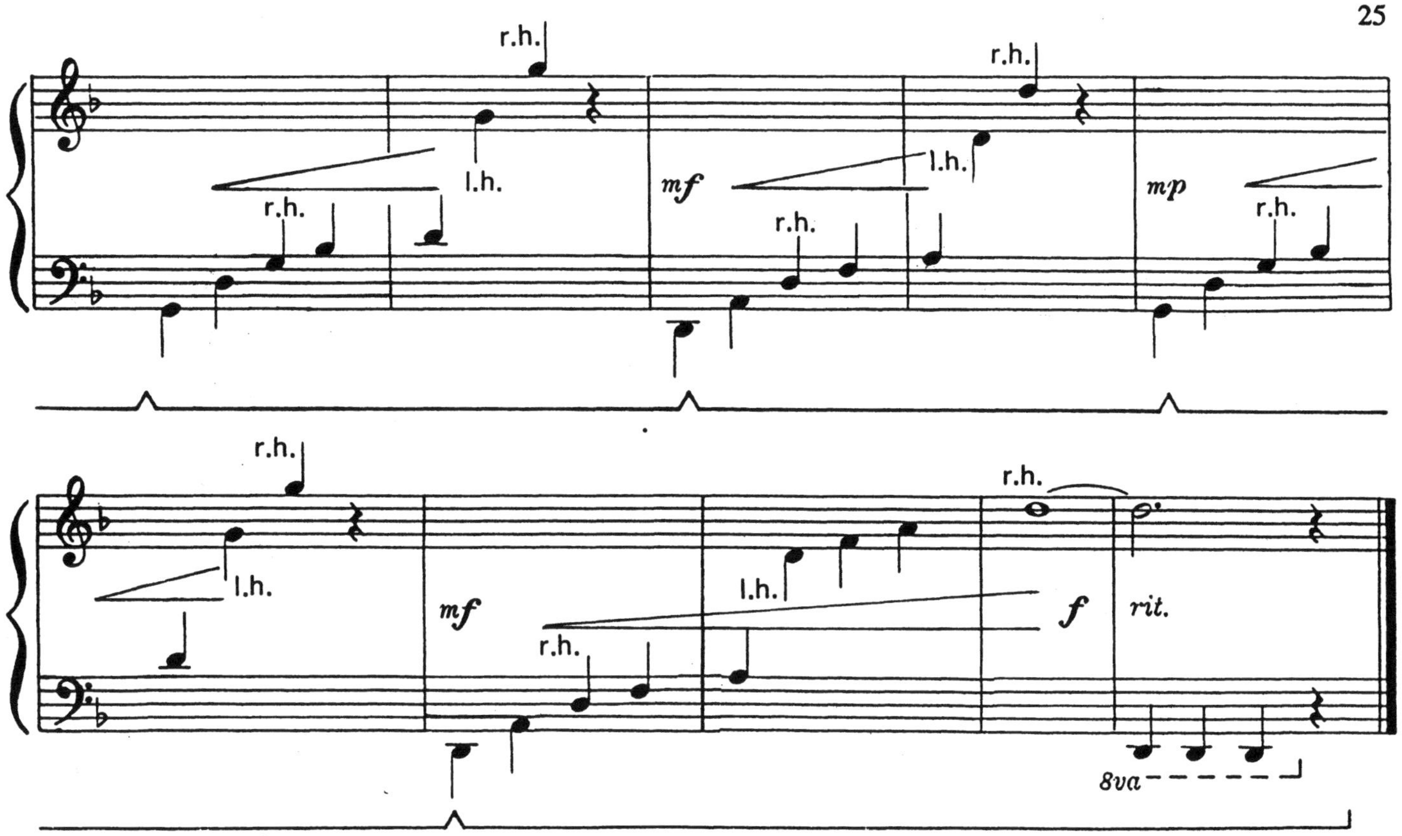

Cathedral Chimes

David Carr Glover

The Merry-Go-Round

David Carr Glover

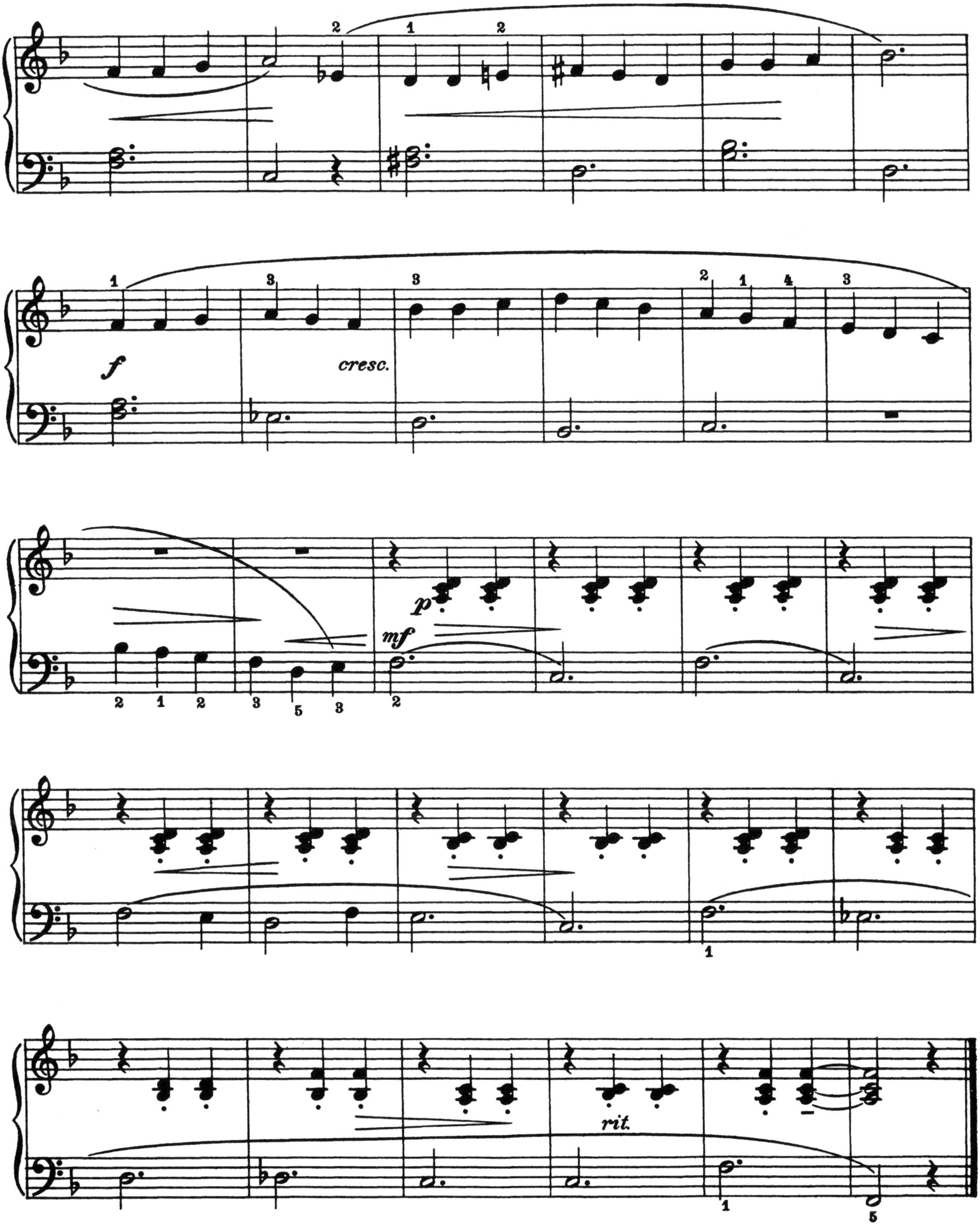
f
cresc.
p
mf
rit.

Rodeo

David Carr Glover

Watch the cow-boy there he goes Do-ing tricks with two las-soes.
cresc.
(girl)
(she)
rit.
Ro-de-o, Ro-de-o, Let's go to the Ro-de-o.
mf atempo
Ev-'ry-one has such fun At the Ro-de-o.
p
pp
ppp
8

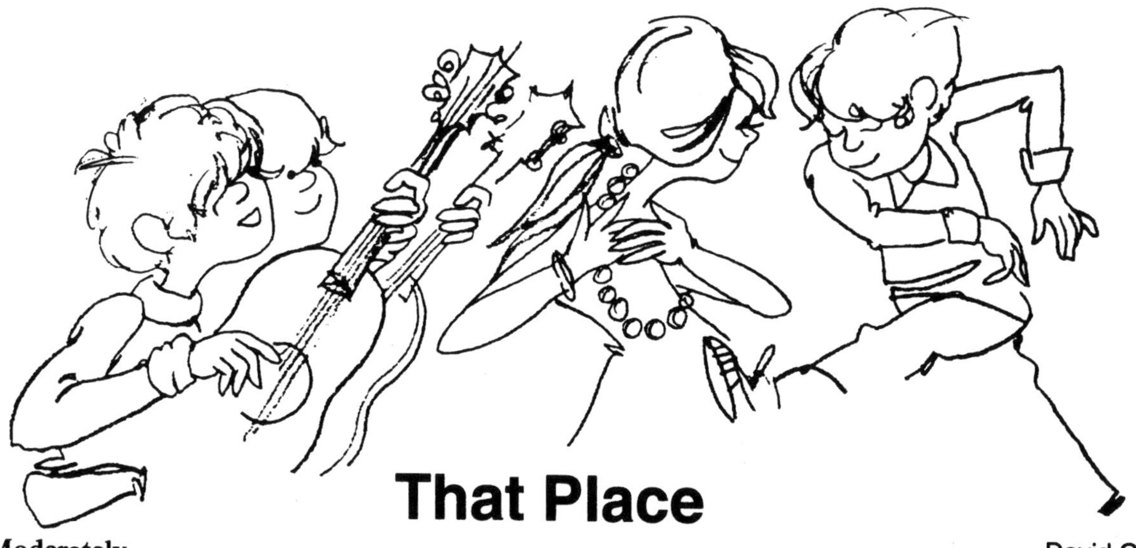

That Place

Moderately

David Carr Glover

mp

mf
p
poco a poco cresc.
ff
8va